EXTRACTS FROM THE WILL OF THE LATE
WILLARD FISKE

―――

―――"I give and bequeath to the Cornell University at Ithaca, New York, all my books relating to Iceland and the old Scandinavian literature and history. . . ."

―――"I give and bequeath to the said Cornell University . . . the sum of Five Thousand (5000) Dollars, to have and to hold for ever, in trust, nevertheless, to receive the income thereof, and to use and expend the said income for the purposes of the publication of an annual volume relating to Iceland and the said Icelandic Collection in the library of the said University."

―――

In pursuance of these provisions the following volumes of ISLANDICA have been issued:

X. Annalium in Islandia farrago and De mirabilibus Islandiæ, by Bishop Gísli Oddsson. Edited by Halldór Hermannsson. 1917.

XI. The Periodical Literature of Iceland down to the year 1874. An historical sketch by Halldór Hermannsson. 1918.

XII. Modern Icelandic. An essay by Halldór Hermannsson. 1919.

XIII. Bibliography of the Eddas, by Halldór Hermannsson. 1920.

XIV. Icelandic Books of the Seventeenth Century, by Halldór Hermannsson. 1922.

XV. Jón Guðmundsson and his Natural History of Iceland, by Halldór Hermannsson. 1924.

XVI. Eggert Ólafsson. A biographical sketch by Halldór Hermannsson. 1925.

XVII. Two Cartographers: Guðbrandur Thorláksson and Thórður Thorláksson, by Halldór Hermannsson. 1926.

XVIII. Sir Joseph Banks and Iceland, by Halldór Hermannsson. 1928.

XIX. Icelandic Manuscripts, by Halldór Hermannsson. 1929.

XX. The Book of the Icelanders (Íslendingabók), by Ari Thorgilsson. Edited and translated, with an introductory essay and notes, by Halldór Hermannsson. 1930.

XXI. The Cartography of Iceland, by Halldór Hermannsson. 1931.

XXII. Sæmund Sigfússon and the Oddaverjar, by Halldór Hermannsson, 1932.

There have also been issued:

CATALOGUE of the Icelandic Collection bequeathed by Willard Fiske. Compiled by Halldór Hermannsson. Ithaca, N. Y., 1914. 4° pp. viii, 755.

——Additions 1913–26. Ithaca, N. Y., 1927. 4° pp. vii, 284.

CATALOGUE of Runic Literature forming a part of the Icelandic Collection bequeathed by Willard Fiske. Compiled by Halldór Hermannsson. Oxford, Oxford University Press, 1917. 4° pp. viii, (2), 106, 1 pl.

ISLANDICA

AN ANNUAL RELATING TO ICELAND

AND THE

FISKE ICELANDIC COLLECTION

IN

CORNELL UNIVERSITY LIBRARY

VOLUME XXIII

OLD ICELANDIC LITERATURE

BY

HALLDÓR HERMANNSSON

ITHACA, NEW YORK
CORNELL UNIVERSITY PRESS
LONDON: HUMPHREY MILFORD
OXFORD UNIVERSITY PRESS
COPENHAGEN: ANDR. FRED. HÖST & SÖN
REYKJAVÍK: BÓKAVERZLUN SIGFÚSAR EYMUNDSSONAR

1933

Old Icelandic Literature

A BIBLIOGRAPHICAL ESSAY

BY

HALLDÓR HERMANNSSON

ITHACA, NEW YORK

CORNELL UNIVERSITY PRESS

LONDON: HUMPHREY MILFORD

OXFORD UNIVERSITY PRESS

1933

LANCASTER PRESS, INC., LANCASTER, PA.

In one of the preceding volumes of the present series I have outlined the external history of Old Icelandic literature as illustrated by the production and the fate of the manuscripts which contain it.[1] In the present volume I propose to sketch in a similar fashion the history of this literature during the age of the printing press, how and where these works were printed and published in the original language and in translations into various tongues. I shall not enumerate all individual editions and translations. This has already been done in the bibliographies which have previously appeared in this series, down to the date of their publication.[2] Of course, much has been added since they saw the light, but it cannot all be mentioned here. What I intend to describe here briefly is the principal agents that have been at work in making these writings accessible in print to scholars and the reading public. This, I hope, will show the interest that has been taken in this literature at various times, and give an indication of the part it has played in certain intellectual movements of different periods during the last three centuries or so. It is not my purpose to trace the writings it has called forth, neither commentaries, nor other philological, historical and literary works, since space will not permit it. At the end I shall draw conclusions as to the principal features of the treatment which this literature has received in the past, and suggest what might be the best plan for carrying on this work in the future.

I. Editing and translating.

I shall deal here principally with serial and collective works and publications of various societies, and I think the most appropriate way to treat them is in groups according to countries, or languages, and to begin with the native land of this literature.

1. ICELAND. Formerly it was commonly assumed that in sixteenth century Iceland the old literature of the country was

---

[1] See *Icelandic Manuscripts* (*Islandica* XIX).

[2] See *Islandica*, vols. I, III–V, XIII; also the two Catalogues of the Fiske Icelandic Collection, of 1914 and 1927.

to a large extent neglected, or forgotten. This doubtless is a somewhat exaggerated view, because we now know that a great many of the early writings were at that time known and read in manuscripts. It is, however, true that an increased interest in the matter was aroused towards the end of the century by the activity of Arngrímur Jónsson who through his Latin works first acquainted foreigners with the existence of this literature. And then immediately requests came from abroad, especially from Denmark, for Icelandic manuscripts, translations, or excerpts from them, in so far as they threw light upon the history of those foreign countries. The requests and other communications from abroad encouraged these studies among the Icelanders. Nothing of this kind, however, was printed there for a long time, except the law code *Jónsbók*, as the press was entirely used in the service of the church. About the middle of the seventeenth century Bishop Brynjólfur Sveinsson of Skálholt conceived the plan of establishing a printing press at his see, to be used solely for the printing of old texts. When he could not carry out this plan, he commenced to send manuscripts to Denmark, hoping that they might be printed there, but even in this he met with disappointment.[1] Throughout the century much study was given to the old literature, although it became increasingly difficult as the years passed, because of the wholesale exportation of the manuscripts to Sweden and Denmark.[2] Under such circumstances it is greatly to Bishop Thórdur Thorláksson's credit that he commissioned Einar Eyjólfsson to search for paper manuscripts which were still left in the country, and prepare these for the printer. Thus during the year 1688 Ari's *Íslendinga-bók* (*Schedæ*), the *Kristni saga*, and the *Landnámabók*, as well as Arngrímur Jónsson's account of the old Greenland colony, were printed at Skálholt, and in the years 1689–91 the large Saga of King Olaf Tryggvason saw the light.[3] Unfortunately the bishop stopped here.

It is not surprising that there was no continuation of this printing at the beginning of the eighteenth century. There were hardly any manuscripts in the country to be printed from, and besides, a certain hostility was to be found among some of the

---

[1] See *Islandica* XIV, pp. vi–vii; XIX, pp. 44–48.

[2] See *Islandica* XIX, pp. 37–71.

[3] See *Islandica* XIV, pp. 4, 52, 61–62, 82–83.

clergy against this pagan literature, as one of the bishops styled it. About the middle of the century, however, there was a revival of interest in it, particularly due to the activities of Eggert Ólafsson,[1] and the first visible results of this were the two collections of sagas which Björn Markússon, the lawman, had printed at Hólar in 1756 under the titles of *Nockrer marg-frooder sögu-þætter Íslendinga,* and *Ágiætar fornmanna sögur* respectively, the first containing nine sagas and tales, the second five sagas. They were doubtless eagerly received and perused by the public, and are now among the great rarities of the Icelandic press.

In 1773 a new press was established in Hrappsey with the avowed purpose of supplying the people with secular literature, but of sagas only two were printed, the Saga of Egil Skalla-grimsson and the spurious Armann Saga, both appearing in 1782. There were plans for publishing others, such as the Laxdæla Saga, the Alexander Saga, and the law-code *Jónsbók,* but these did not materialize. The press, however, issued several *rímur* of modern origin dealing with subjects mainly drawn from the Mythical-heroic Sagas.[2]

The Hrappsey Press ultimately passed under the control of the newly founded Icelandic Society for National Enlightenment (*Landsuppfræðingarjélag*)[3] whose aim and spirit were rather unfavorable to the cultivation of the early national traditions. Under its auspices only one volume of Snorri Sturlason's *Heims-kringla* appeared (1804). The only other publication of a similar character which the Icelandic press of that period published on its own initiative was an edition of the Saga of Njal (1844)—in modern spelling!

Yet the people were beginning to take a greater interest than ever before in their past history and literature, and this was encouraged by similar movements abroad. It, among other things, was the cause of the foundation of the Icelandic Literary Society (*Bókmentafélag*) in 1816,[4] but most of this society's publications in the field of the old literature, although prepared and edited by Icelanders, were printed in Denmark, and will

---

[1] See *Islandica* XVI.

[2] See Jón Helgason, *Hrappseyjarprentsmiðja 1773–1794.* Kaupmannahöfn 1928.

[3] See *Islandica* XI, p. 16 ff.

[4] See *Islandica* XI, p. 26 ff.

therefore be dealt with under that country.   The only works of that character which the Society has published in Iceland are a fragment of the *Hauksbók*, B. M. Ólsen's edition of the *Sólarljóð* (1915), and the unfinished collection of medieval poems which Jón Thorkelsson started (*Kvæðasafn*, 1922–27).

Within the country the Latin School at Bessastadir and afterwards in Reykjavík, was, from the third decade of the nineteenth century until the foundation of the University of Iceland early in the present century, the centre for the study of the national literature.   Sveinbjörn Egilsson was the pioneer in this work, but most of his writings were issued under the auspices of the Society of Northern Antiquaries in Copenhagen, as will be mentioned below.   Only a few of his editions were printed in Iceland as annual programs of the school, the most important being that of the Prose Edda with the Grammatical Treatises (1848–49).   The programs issued by his successors have been chiefly of an exegetic and lexicographical character.[1]

About the middle of the nineteenth century a new printing press was established at Akureyri.   One of its early directors, Sveinn Skúlason, evidently planned the publication of sagas and other early writings.   He began a series which he called *Íslendinga sögur*, but only two volumes appeared containing the Vatnsdæla Saga (1858) and the Finnboga Saga (1860).   Possibly the Laxdæla Saga of 1867 was intended as one of them, although it has no serial title.   About that time began also sporadic printing by various Icelandic presses of the late fictitious sagas, and between 1852 and 1911 about twenty-five of these sagas appeared. This is easy to explain.   They were still popular, and manuscripts of them were to be found in the country.

In the late seventies and early nineties a few of the shorter Sagas of Icelanders were also published, such as the sagas of the Sons of Droplaug (1878), of Gull-Thorir (1878), of Gunnlaug (1880), and of the Floamenn (1884).   The last one, an unusually handsome volume, was published by Sigmundur Gudmundsson, an enterprising printer who conceived a plan to print a new edition of the *Fornaldarsögur Norðrlanda*, largely a re-issue of Rafn's well-known collection.   After the publication of the first volume (1885) his firm passed into the hands of Sigurdur Kristjánsson who published the last two volumes (1886–89).   The

---

[1] Cf. *Islandica* XI, pp. 35–37.

latter planned a collective edition of fictitious sagas under the title of *Ævintýrasögur*, but only two small parts saw the light, containing Erex' Saga and Ingvar's Saga (1886).

The difficulty of obtaining the Sagas of Icelanders was keenly felt by the people. The Kings' Sagas were not so very scarce, since copies of the *Fornmanna sögur* were still to be found in many places, but to get hold of many of the family sagas was next to impossible, yet in them people were most interested. Sigurdur Kristjánsson, a farsighted and patriotic publisher, saw here his opportunity and decided to publish all the Sagas of Icelanders in a uniform series, called *Íslendinga sögur*, and this he accomplished in thirty-eight small handy volumes during the years between 1892 and 1902.[1] Valdimar Ásmundsson, a self-made man and journalist, edited the whole series. The edition is of a popular character, and is based not on the manuscripts but on other editions. It was of inestimable value thus to give the people easy access to this literature. Many of the volumes have gone through two or three editions, usually revised by Benedikt Sveinsson. Then followed *Fjörutíu Íslendinga þættir* (1904), edited by Thorleifur Jónsson, a collection of tales about Icelanders, which are to be found inserted in the King's Sagas, the two Eddas (1905 and 1907) edited by Finnur Jónsson, and finally the Saga of the Sturlungs in four volumes (1908–15) edited by Björn Bjarnason and Benedikt Sveinsson. An edition of Snorri's *Heimskringla*, published by another firm in Reykjavík (1892–93), was, on the other hand, never completed.

In 1911 the University of Iceland was established with a chair of Icelandic literature and language; this has since been divided into two, one of literature, the other of language. Needless to say that this arrangement has done much to further these studies. The University publishes programs annually, and among them have appeared an edition of Stuf's Saga (1912) by B. M. Ólsen, and one of the *Völuspá* (1923) by Sigurdur Nordal, undoubtedly the best of this famous poem.

It was realized that the edition of the *Íslendinga sögur* mentioned above would not in the long run satisfy the Icelandic public; besides it contained only that one group of sagas. More critical and more elaborate edition of all the principal literary

---

[1] See *Catalogue of the Fiske Icel. Coll.*, 1914, pp. 270–71.

monuments, with notes and explanations, was needed.　This led
to the formation of The Icelandic Old Text Society (*Hið íslenzka
Fornritafélag*) which was founded June 14, 1928.[1]　Its object is
to publish an elaborate edition of all the principal works of the
Old Icelandic literature, with the aid of various editors, each work
to be provided with an introduction giving an estimate of its
literary, historical and linguistic value; moreover, with annotations, explanations of verses, of unusual words and phrases, and
of ancient customs and practices.　The chronology will be discussed, and references given to and comparisons made with other
works.　Maps illustrating the scene of each saga will be included,
genealogical tables, and pictures of places, houses, old instruments
and other antiquities.　The edition is to form thirty-two volumes,
the various works being grouped together according to their
literary or geographical relationship.　To cover the initial
expenses a fund has been collected, partly from private indi-
viduals, partly supported by public grants, and this, according
to the last available report (1931),[2] amounts to 57,000 Krónur.
The first volume was to appear in 1930, but has just been
published, containing Egil Skallagrimsson's Saga.　It is to be
hoped that the plan will meet with success; the funds are not
ample, and much will depend upon the sale of the volumes.
There are still many difficulties to contend with in preparing
and printing such works in Iceland.　The important manuscripts are to be found elsewhere, and it is planned to base the
edition directly upon the manuscripts.　These have therefore
either to be borrowed and brought to Iceland, or journeys made
by the editors to consult them.　Furthermore, literary facilities
are not good there, and many books needed in preparing the
edition may not always be at hand.　The directors of the Society
are, however, determined to make the edition as good as possible,
but it is to be expected that it will take a long time to complete it.
Although it is intended principally for Icelandic readers, foreigners interested in this literature will doubtless find it indis-
pensable.

[1] See *Hið íslenzka Fornritafélag 1928. Stofnskrá, lög, efnisskrá.* Reykjavík
1928, 8°, pp. 12.—Cf. also *Vaka* II, 1928, pp. 9–16.

[2] *Hið íslenzka Fornritafélag 1929–30. Skýrsla, reikningar, félagatal.* Reykjavík 1931, 8°, pp. 16.

2. DENMARK. As mentioned above the interest which the Danes first showed in Old Icelandic literature was due to their desire for information about their own early history. But for some time nothing of what was brought from Iceland was published. The first Icelandic texts to appear in print were the *Krákumál* and Egil Skallagrimsson's *Höfuðlausn*, which were included in Ole Worm's *Danica litteratura antiquissima* (1636), and they were printed in Runic characters.[1] Worm's deep interest in this literature did much to spur the Icelanders to devote themselves to the study of it. The time, however, was not yet ripe for the printing of it on a large scale.

The importance of publishing these texts was first emphasized by Bishop Brynjólfur Sveinsson, and for two reasons, first, that the manuscripts were few, many of them in a precarious condition, and thus the texts might be lost; secondly, that these works were of such a character that they deserved to be given a wider circulation than the manuscripts afforded, and thus enhance the prestige of the nation which had produced them. The bishop's arguments fell on deaf ears, and practically nothing was done to carry out the plan he recommended. Partly the jealousy of some of the bishop's countrymen, partly the indifference of the Danish king and his advisers are to be blamed for this. All that was printed, was a little pamphlet containing a short tale of a Norwegian king, translated into Latin by the king's antiquary (1658).[2] The only old Icelandic texts which were printed in Denmark during the seventeenth century were published at the instance of Peder H. Resen, a great collector of books and manuscripts and withal a man of learning. He issued in 1665 an edition of the Prose Edda with a long introduction and Danish and Latin translations. The text was that prepared by Rev. Magnús Ólafsson of Laufás, and hence generally known as the *Laufás Edda*. In the same year Resen published the *Völuspá* and the *Hávamál* in separate volumes, the editions being the work of two Icelanders.[3] At the order of the king Torfæus had for a long time been occupied with translating many of the sagas, but none of his translations were printed. In his numerous historical works written in Latin he drew upon this

---

[1] Cf. *Islandica* XIX, p. 1.
[2] Cf. *Islandica* XIV, p. 40.
[3] Cf. *Islandica* XIV, pp. 96–97, 109, 41.

literature, in fact some of his works are little more than translations or paraphrases of certain sagas. Thus the contents of many sagas became known to the learned world through his pen. In the earlier half of the eighteenth century no texts were printed except Bussæus' edition of Ari's *Schedæ* (1744).

It took the Danes a long time to place the Arna-Magnæan Foundation upon a working basis. A charter was finally signed by the king in 1760, but there was still a delay of a dozen years before any publishing was started.[1] The provisions in the charter regarding this were as follows: For publishing were to be chosen, first the most reliable, best, and most useful works in the collection, and thereafter those of less value; of the fabulous or fictitious works only extracts or abstracts which threw light upon Northern antiquities might be published. When no more works worth publishing could be found in the Arna-Magnæan Collection, the Commission was at liberty to choose for publication other old manuscripts, or writings within the same field. The publications were to be printed on good white paper, in clear, good type, and to be sold to the public at as low a price as possible. Every year, or every other year at least, something was to be issued in print. The first text issued by the so-called Arna-Magnæan Commission was the *Kristni saga* in 1772. In the same year there appeared Olavius' edition of Njal's Saga, which was later acquired by the Commission, and which for a century was the only usable edition of this famous saga, and is still in print although few know it. In 1773 the *Hungrvaka* together with some others appeared, in 1775 Gunnlaug's Saga, in 1780 the *Rímbegla*, in 1785 Hervör's Saga, in 1786 the Saga of Viga-Glum, and in 1787 the Eyrbyggja Saga; the last four were published at the expense of P. F. Suhm, the Danish historian, and turned over to the Commission. The editing of them all was done by Icelanders residing in Copenhagen; a Latin translation accompanied the Icelandic text in every case. In the meantime the Commission had decided to publish the Poetic Edda; great preparations were made for the edition and some people in Iceland were consulted. All this took time, and the progress of publishing was also inordinately slow. The first volume saw the light in 1787, the second in 1818, and the third and last in 1828. Forty years proved too long waiting for people

---

[1] See *Islandica* XIX, p. 67 ff.

who were really interested in this work, and they had also in the meantime been provided with two partial editions and one complete from other sources. The Edda edition was, however, so costly that the Commission could publish little else. Yet Egil's Saga appeared in 1809 and a Latin translation of Njal's Saga; in 1826 the Laxdæla Saga was published. In 1829 the *Grágás* was printed, in 1832 Kormak's Saga, in 1847 the *Járnsíða*, and an edition of the Icelandic Annals. In 1848 the first volume of the Prose Edda appeared, the beginning of an undertaking which was destined to take forty years to complete, since the last part of the third volume appeared in 1887. During this period a few other books were issued, such as a facsimile edition of the *Elucidarius* (1869), and an edition of two different recensions of the *Grágás* (the *Staðarhólsbók*, 1879, and the *Skálholtsbók*, 1883), both edited by Vilh. Finsen. For some time after this the activities of the Commission were devoted to the printing of the long-looked-for catalogue of the manuscript collection, which was followed by a *Palæographical Atlas* (published at the expense of the Carlsberg Fund). An edition of the skaldic poetry (*Den norsk-islandske Skjaldedigtning*) took eight years (1908–15), and the texts published since that time include the *Melabók* recension of the *Landnámabók* (1921, without indices of places and persons), Alexander's Saga (1924), and a new edition with critical apparatus of the Prose Edda (1931). All these works have been published in a rather limited number of copies and because of the peculiar policy followed by the Commission throughout its existence have had but a small circulation. But more about this below.

With the rise of Romanticism there was a growing demand for the saga literature. The Danish reigning house showed its interest in it by supporting a stately edition of the Kings' Sagas which was finished in the course of fifty years (1777–1826). We may assume that that was a period when people had inexhaustible patience to wait, so the editors were in no hurry to complete their task. Unfortunately this dilatory method has in some cases survived into our own time in the field of this literature, as we may have occasion to mention further on.

The aim of the Icelandic Literary Society (*Bókmentafélag*) which was founded in 1816 with a branch in Copenhagen, was to further Icelandic studies of all kinds; thus the old literature

fell within its field as well as the modern. Accordingly the
Copenhagen branch issued the Saga of the Sturlungs in two
volumes (1817–20). This course, however, was abandoned as
another society which we shall presently deal with, was started
which had the old literature for its particular field. Only when
that society relaxed its efforts in this respect, the Literary
Society turned again to the old literature and issued two volumes
of *Biskupa sögur* (1858–78), and three volumes of *Íslenzkar
fornsögur* (1880–83), the latter containing six sagas. For the
second time its activity in this field was discontinued, presumably
because at that time another society was founded in Copenhagen
which was to devote itself to this literature. The last works
which the Copenhagen branch published in this line were Ari's
Íslendingabók (1887), and a collection of four *Rímur* (1896).

The dilatory and impractical methods of the Arna-Magnæan
Commission and its inability to satisfy the demand for the sagas,
was one of the principal reasons for the foundation of *Det
nordiske Oldskrift-Selskab*, known in English under the name
of Society of Northern Antiquaries (afterwards with the epithet
of Royal). It was founded in 1825 by four men, the Dane Carl
Chr. Rafn, and the three Icelanders, Sveinbjörn Egilsson, Gísli
Brynjúlfsson, and Thorgeir Gudmundsson. The first two soon
afterwards left Copenhagen and returned to Iceland, where
Sveinbjörn, however, continued his work for the Society, while
Thorgeir some years later severed his connections with it. That
left Rafn in control as the permanent secretary for the rest of
his life. And a very efficient one he was. He was the most
industrious and practical of men, a clear-headed business man,
who knew how to interest people in the enterprise, and secure
a wide circulation for the publications. From the start the output
was large, and the growth of the Society's fund rapid. Contributions were received from all countries, from Siam in the East,
to America in the West. Rafn was an indefatigable corre-
spondent and knew how to approach and win men of power and
wealth. In 1834 the permanent fund amounted to 12,500
Rigsdaler, in 1845 it had become 46,000 Rigsdaler, and about
twenty years later at the time of Rafn's death it was 84,500
Rigsdaler. Most of this sum had been collected abroad, because
contributions from Denmark amounted only to 7,950 Rigsdaler.
And the fund was collected for the purpose of carrying out the
object of the Society as expressed in the by-laws.

The principal object of the Society according to the by-laws and the numerous circulars it sent out, was "the publication of Old Icelandic manuscripts and of other Old Northern literary remains. Its plan, however, comprehends besides whatever else may serve to throw light upon the ancient history, the language, and the antiquities in general of the North." In order to carry this out, "the ancient writings are," the circular continues, "published in the original text, and also in translations in Danish, Latin, or one of the most extensively used modern languages. By publishing this triple series of works the Society aims, at once, at cherishing in Iceland itself that fondness for the national literature which has there prevailed for centuries; at giving to the people of the North in general readier access to the chief sources of their country's early history; and at placing within reach of the literary men of other countries a body of ancient writings replete with matter illustrative of their history, language, or antiquities." The publications here referred to are the *Fornmanna sögur* (a rather indefinite title, the series covering principally the Kings' Sagas) in twelve volumes (1825–37), with a Danish translation, *Oldnordiske Sagaer* (another unfortunate title), in the same number of volumes (1826–37), and a Latin version by Svbj. Egilsson, *Scripta historica Islandorum de rebus gestis veterum Borealium* (1828–46). Then there was a three volume edition of Mythical-heroic Sagas with the title *Fornaldarsögur Norðrlanda* (1829–30), also with a Danish translation, *Nordiske Fortids Sagaer* (1829–30), a rendering which Rafn had previously, in a slightly different form, published at his own expense under the title *Nordiske Kæmpehistorier* (1821–26, 3 vols.). A similar series of the Sagas of Icelanders was planned and begun, *Íslendinga sögur*, of which two volumes were printed (1829–30). This, however, turned out badly and was discontinued, but a Danish translation of the ten most important of these sagas, by N. M. Petersen, was published, entitled *Historiske Fortællinger om Islændernes Færd hjemme og ude* (1839–44, in four volumes) which became very popular with Danish readers. Another series of the original texts was started under the same title, *Íslendinga sögur*, and two volumes, edited by Jón Sigurdsson, were printed (1843–47); the next volume was to contain Njal's Saga, edited by Konrád Gíslason, but it took him thirty years to prepare the text (1875) and fourteen more to finish the commentary (1889). Such dilly-dallying killed the plan, besides in the meantime changes had been brought about within the Society.

A work in three volumes, *Grönlands historiske Mindesmærker* (1838–45), covered the history of the Icelandic colony in Greenland, and the texts relating to the early discovery of the American continent were printed in a stately quarto volume entitled *Antiquitates Americanæ* (1837), Rafn's trump card to arouse the interest of Americans in the Society and its program. This was followed by *Antiquités Russes* (1850–52), two big folio volumes, containing the sources of the relations between Eastern Europe and the Northern countries. A similar work was planned covering the Norse-Icelandic sources of British history, but this was never published. Divergences of policy were at that time coming to the fore within the Society.

The Society had in those years displayed a tremendous activity, in which Rafn was the moving spirit. The big contributions to the fund from abroad show how deep interest was taken in the work there. The large fund thus collected became a great temptation to some members of the Society. There was developing a school of archæology in Denmark under the leadership of J. J. A. Worsaae, and this group within the Society thought that enough had now been done for Icelandic literature, and that it was time to turn to other things with the aid of the fund. Rafn opposed this, and no changes were made so long as he lived. But no sooner was he dead (1864) than Worsaae began to push his plans for changing the by-laws and regulations for the fund, in interest of prehistoric archæology. Jón Sigurdsson, the Icelandic scholar, opposed this, and it was maintained by many that such changes constituted a breach of faith towards the donors, many of whom were then still alive; it would be to use the fund for other purposes than those for which it was intended, and that was at least unethical. Worsaae and his followers were in majority, overrode the opposition, and made changes to favor their activities.[1] There were to be two sections within

---

[1] Cf. Jón Sigurðsson, *Bréf*, 1911, pp. 368–72, 381–83; Páll E. Ólason, *Jón Sigurðsson*, IV, 1932, pp. 33–38. It is regrettable that the history of the Society has never been written. One might have expected that this would have been done on the occasion of its centenary (1925). The board of directors, however, did not see fit to do so. Instead they celebrated the anniversary by publishing a new edition of the *Landnámabók* with the imprint of the Society, but at the expense of the Carlsberg Fund!

the Society, one literary, the other archæological, each with its secretary. Nominally they were to divide the income equally between them, but it is obvious from the annual financial reports since the change took place that the archæological section has taken the lion's share. For the next thirty years hardly any old texts were printed, but then that work was revived to a certain extent. The *Hauksbók* was published (1892–96), followed by an edition of three recensions of the *Landnámabók* (1900), another of the same work (1925) where these recensions were worked into a whole, and a few other texts (the Saga of the Faroese, 1927, and Gisli's Saga, 1929), all edited by Finnur Jónsson. Most important, however, is Kaalund's critical edition of the *Sturlunga saga* with a Danish translation (1906–11). Some of these and other works, although bearing the imprint of the Society, have been published with funds derived from other sources.

Dissatisfaction with the work of the Arna-Magnæan Commission and with the expensive and somewhat spectacular publications of the Society of Northern Antiquaries led to the foundation in 1847 of a new society, called *Det nordiske Litteratur-Samfund*. The founders were N. M. Petersen and several Icelanders residing in Copenhagen. Its object was to disseminate knowledge of the Old Northern literature through the publication of texts, chiefly Icelandic, in a manner which made them accessible to a wider circle of readers, and to provide them with Danish translations. It met with a good reception, and the membership rose to about 400, but after working for about a quarter of a century, the organization was dissolved, or at least ceased publishing, for what reason I do not know, presumably for lack of support. It kept various works going at the same time, publishing them in parts, so that it often took several years until a work was finished. They were issued in small octavo, under the general title of *Nordiske Oldskrifter* representing on the whole good critical texts. They include some thirteen Sagas of Icelanders, and Icelandic medieval ballads. Because of the Danish translation on the opposite page, they probably found small sale outside of Denmark. The most important work in the series is the diplomatic edition of the *Codex regius* of the *Grágás*, with a Danish translation, by Vilhj. Finsen (1850–70).

In 1879 another society of a similar constitution was formed in

Copenhagen, called *Samfund til Udgivelse af gammel nordisk Litteratur*, a very long and inconvenient name. Its by-laws state the aim of the Society as being "to bring to light and publish Northern literary products of earlier periods." To it were transferred the publications of its predecessor. It can now look upon a useful activity of more than half a century, its publications numbering nearly sixty volumes, of which more than forty represent Icelandic texts, all critical editions, with variants, the most noteworthy among them being the *Heimskringla* (1893–1901), the four Grammatical Treatises (1884–86), *Alfræði íslenzk* (1908–18), a collection of early *Rímur* with a glossary (1905–28), and facsimile editions of the *Codex regius* of the Poetic Edda (1890) and of another Edda manuscript (1896). It is an unwritten law in the Society that no one but Scandinavians can be accepted as editors, certainly a narrow and mistaken principle. Among the editors of Icelandic texts are eight Icelanders, eight Swedes, three Danes, two Norwegians, and one Faroese.[1] The Society has received support from the Danish government and from other public funds. Its membership represents, however, a curious phase. It rose in the first year to some 330 members at home and abroad but soon fell and has usually hovered around 250, indicating, as it seems, that the Society has not lived up to what was expected of it at the start. This probably is chiefly due to its method of publishing; it keeps many works going at the same time, publishing them in small annual parts, so it may take years before the whole work is printed. To mention an example from its most recent publications, the edition of the *Morkinskinna*, a book of some 500 pages, appeared in five parts during the years 1928–32. Such a method is not likely to arouse interest in, or enthusiasm for, the subject; it is most conducive to weariness. It is a plan which may have worked well a hundred years ago, although I doubt it; it is now entirely out of date. It is possible to distribute the parts to members, but those works cannot be put on the market, since they come dribbling in small parts over a period of several years. The Society might take a new lease of life, if this anachronism was abandoned.

It was often customary to insert in the early editions a

---

[1] Finnur Jónsson has twelve editions to his credit, Kr. Kaalund eight, others fewer.

facsimile page of the principal manuscript. This was in the beginning usually engraved on copper, neat looking, but not always very accurate. Later it was shown in photolithography, and gradually some smaller works were reproduced in this way, as for instance the *Elucidarius* (1869) and the *Physiologus* (1889), both consisting of only a few pages. Finally the photographic method was employed as in the two Edda facsimile editions (1890 and 1896) mentioned above. The process was expensive, but soon the method was improved upon, made easier and less costly. It is surprising that more frequent use has not been made of it in later years for reproduction of Icelandic manuscripts. It was reserved for an enterprising and farsighted publisher to conceive such a plan and carry it out on a large scale. Mr. Ejnar Munksgaard of the publishing house of Levin & Munksgaard, Copenhagen, realized the value of such publications, and in 1930 issued the first volume of his *Corpus Codicum Islandicorum Medii Ævi*, consisting of the *Flateyjarbók*, the largest Icelandic vellum codex of the Middle Ages now in existence. The edition was published in commemoration of the millennium of the Icelandic Parliament, and a most impressive and welcome memorial it was to the Icelandic nation. It was followed in 1931 by the *Codex Wormianus* of the Prose Edda, and in 1932 the *Codex regius* of the *Grágás*, and the *Codex Frisianus* of the Kings' Sagas appeared. Other codices are in preparation. Each volume is provided with an introduction by different writers. The reproductions are in the natural size of the manuscripts, very clear and in every respect satisfactory, and the whole make-up of the volumes most attractive. This is, without doubt, the most important undertaking in the history of this literature, because it makes it possible for scholars in all parts of the world to become acquainted with these texts as they appear in the manuscripts, and thus to make independent studies of them without having to travel far to consult the originals; and I feel sure that it will revive widespread interest in this literature and encourage research. Besides, it is of paramount importance to have such exact reproductions if anything should happen to the originals, in case of fire or other calamities. In fact, it may well be assumed, that this enterprise will initiate a new epoch with regard to these studies.

The early editions were most frequently provided with a

Danish, or a Latin translation, or both. Separate translations also appeared, as for instance K. L. Rahbek's *Nordiske Fortællinger* (1819–21, 2 vols.) containing Njal's Saga and various minor tales. N. F. S. Grundtvig translated the *Heimskringla* (1813–22), a rendering which in spite of its numerous instances of colloquialisms and solecisms went through three editions. We have already referred to the collections of translations published by the Society of Northern Antiquaries. And there were others of a similar kind. Brynjólfur Snorrason and Kristian Arentzen translated a number of the shorter sagas which were published in four volumes (*Sagaer*, 1849–50). Fred. Winkel Horn translated nineteen Sagas of Icelanders which appeared in a collection entitled *Billeder af Livet paa Island* (1871–76, 3 vols.) and he also rendered six Mythical-heroic Sagas, which are to be found in his *Nordiske Heltesagaer* (1876). None of these translations seems to have attained popularity, as no new edition appeared. This, however, fell to the lot of N. M. Petersen's translation in *Historiske Fortællinger*, mentioned above. After having been taken over by a publishing house it went through three editions. It doubtless is a meritorious work, but now in many respects out of date. Its shortcomings were recently pointed out by Gunnar Gunnarsson, the novelist, and his criticism of it led to a controversy [1] which finally resulted in the formation of the Society for Publishing Icelandic Sagas in Danish (*Selskabet til Udgivelse af islandske Sagaer*, 1927), which found immediate support from various sides, and financial aid from public funds. The translating was undertaken by some of the best known names in Danish literature of to-day, and a prominent Danish artist, Johannes Larsen, was sent to Iceland to prepare illustrations for the work. It was planned to form three volumes, and was to be published in parts; the first part appeared early in 1930, and the twenty-first and last at the beginning of the present year, making in all over one thousand pages in large quarto. It was quickly and to all appearances well done. The volumes include fourteen Sagas of Icelanders, with illustrations, maps, and genealogical tables, each volume having an introduction on themes connected with this literature, by Joh. V. Jensen, Gunnar Gunnarsson, and Vilh. Andersen respectively. The

---

[1] This controversy was carried on in the columns of the Copenhagen daily *Politiken* during Dec. 1926 and Jan. 1927.

translations, being by different hands, are not all of the same character, they often bear the individual stamp of their authors. So far as I have observed they are on the whole of a high quality, and make a noteworthy contribution to the history of this literature. The edition is expensive and will therefore hardly attain a wide circulation, or be in a position to supplant the Petersen translation, of which there are cheap editions. If, however, it finds favor with Danish readers, we may expect that a popular edition will soon follow.

3. NORWAY. The country which next to Iceland contributed the largest share to the medieval literature of the North, was for a long time in a similar position to that of Iceland with regard to facilities for printing the old texts. Besides, linguistic changes which had taken place there brought it about that the Norwegian people were no longer able to read this literature in the original. In sixteenth century Norway there were still a few men, the so-called lawmen, who understood the old tongue, and it is from their pens that the earliest translations of the Kings' Sagas emanated. These, however, together with most of the manuscripts, found their way sooner or later to Denmark, where some of them were printed, like P. Claussön Friis' version which was edited by Ole Worm and printed in 1633. There were a few Norwegians during the eighteenth century who made a study of the old literature, but most of them lived and worked in Denmark, like Gerhard Schöning who was one of the editors of the Kings' Sagas published under royal auspices which has been mentioned above.

After the separation of Norway from Denmark in 1814, the rising national feeling made the Norwegians turn their attention to the literature of their ancestors. The leader of that part of the national movement was Jacob Rudolf Keyser who in the twenties of the nineteenth century went to Iceland, and spent two years there with Sveinbjörn Egilsson in order to study the Icelandic tongue. His pupils and co-workers were Peter A. Munch and Carl Unger who were destined to edit many of the old texts, especially the latter who lived longest of the two, and was a prolific and painstaking editor. Some of these works were published by various publishing firms, such as Alexander's Saga (1848), the *Stjörn* (1862), the Poetic Edda, edited by Munch

(1846) and that epoch making edition of the same work by Sophus Bugge (1856). Many were issued as programs of the national university, like the *Fagrskinna* (1847), St. Olaf's Saga (1853), Olaf Tryggvason's Saga (1853), the *Morkinskinna* (1867), Thomas' Saga (1869), the Sagas of the Apostles (1874), the Sagas of the Saints (1877), and others.

In 1857 the *Kildeskriftfond* was established with government subsidy, which later was changed to the *Kommissionen til Udgivelse af Kildeskrifter til Norges Historie* (1886). This institution undertook the publication of various old texts. Among them are the *Flateyjarbók* (1859–60, 3 vols.), the *Codex Frisianus* (1871), Icelandic Annals, edited by Gustav Storm (1888), Odd's Saga of Olaf Tryggvason (1895), the *Eirspennill* (1916), the *Skálholtsbók*, containing the Sagas of King Sverrir and his successors (1910–26), and a recension of St. Olaf's Saga (1922).

In 1861 *Det norske Oldskriftselskab* was founded with the aim of publishing Old Norse (*norrøne*) writings, and other works elucidating the early history of the Norwegian people. It ceased publishing 1873, but was not really dissolved until 1890. Among its publications are Gunnlaug's Saga (1862), the *Heimskringla* (1864–68), *Maríu saga* (1867–71), the *Eirspennill* (partial edition, 1870–73), and an unfinished edition by S. Bugge of some Mythical-heroic Sagas (1863–73). The remainder of these publications was turned over to the *Kildeskriftkommission*.

The Norwegian Academy of Sciences in Oslo has published very few Old Icelandic works. They are: Laurents Hanssön's translation of the Kings' Sagas (1899), the *Sólarljóð* (1914), the very interesting Icelandic Sketch-book (1910), and a Medical Miscellany (1931).

It may be mentioned that the works published in Norway were edited by Norwegians, except the *Flateyjarbók* which Gudbr. Vigfusson edited in collaboration with Unger, and the later edition of the *Eirspennill*, which was edited by Finnur Jónsson.

As to translations it is but natural that these should be largely of works dealing with Norway, that is above all the Kings' Sagas. The first of these to appear in print in Norway was Jacob Aall's translation of all the Kings' Sagas (1838–39) in three stately volumes with important geographical annotations by G. Munthe and attractive steel engravings of historical sites. P. A. Munch apparently intended to publish a translation series of the Icelandic sagas, under the title of *Sagaer eller Fortællinger om Nordmænds og Islænderes Bedrifter i Oldtiden*, but only two small volumes saw the light (Gisli's Saga, and the Saga of Hen-Thorir, 1845). He was already at that time busy with a translation of the Kings' Sagas which was completed after his death by O. Rygh (1859–71). This rendering was not found quite satisfactory, hence Gustav Storm prepared a new one of the *Heimskringla* which was first published in a handsome quarto volume with numerous illustrations by Norwegian artists (1899); a popular octavo edition followed in the next year, together with one in the popular idiom (*Landsmaalet*) by Stener Schjøtt. A handsome four volume translation of all the Kings' Sagas by G. Storm and Alex. Bugge, was published in 1914 commemorating the centenary of the separation of the country from Denmark. It includes the illustrations of Storm's translation.

Of other saga translations, the one, partly selections from and paraphrases of various sagas by Gerhard Gran, edited by N. Rolfsen and issued under the title *Vore Fædres Værk* (1888), deserves mention, especially the second edition (1889) which has good illustrations by A. Bloch. O. A. Överland translated and paraphrased six Icelandic sagas in his series *Historiske Fortællinger* (1896–97), and Alex. Bugge a few in his volume *Udvalgte Sagaer* (1901). During the last decade a series of translations of the principal family sagas was begun, and some prominent writers were engaged for the task, among them Sigrid Undset, Fredrik Paasche, and others. The serial title is *Islandske Ættesagaer*, and seven volumes were issued during the years 1922–28, including Njal's Saga, Laxdæla Saga, Eyrbyggja Saga, and seven others. They were issued under the auspices of an organization called *Riksmaalsvernet* and published by Aschehoug & Co. During the last four years no new volumes have appeared, so probably the series has been discontinued. Altogether it is attractive publications and very handsomely made up.

The translations we have so far dealt with are in the official literary language, the Dano-Norwegian, or *Riksmaalet*, but there are others in the popular language, or *Landsmaalet*, which since the middle of the last century has been fighting for recognition. Into this language many sagas have been rendered, a number of which had first appeared in some provincial paper, and were then reprinted. Among the earliest of these translations is Schjøtt's rendering of the *Heimskringla* (1874–79), the third edition of which was referred to above. A branch (*Landsmaalslaget*) of a society called *Det norske samlaget*, has for the last quarter of a century (since 1907) published a series entitled *Gamalnorske bokverk* (Old Norwegian writings) which consist almost entirely of translations of Icelandic sagas, some of them with the original text (styled here *gamalnorsk grunntekst*). The translations are by different hands and now number some thirty volumes, and no doubt the close relationship between the two languages makes translating easy. Noticeable is especially Ivar Mortensen's translation of the Poetic Edda, which is very neatly made up in a large quarto volume, while the rest is in small octavo. The serial title has caused irritation among the Icelanders, not without reason, because it seems meant to convey the erroneous impression that these are Norwegian writings, while almost all of them are in fact Icelandic. Seemingly the publishers have finally realized the errors of their way in this respect, and with volume twenty-three changed the serial title to *Norrøne bokverk* which is more appropriate.[1]

4. SWEDEN. At the time when the Icelandic manuscripts arrived in Sweden, a strong nationalistic movement prevailed there after the Swedish successes in the Thirty Years War and after their triumph over the Danes in 1658. The Swedish scholars eagerly scanned the Icelandic writings for information about their early history, and they thought they found it especially in the Mythical-heroic Sagas. Hence it was that these particularly held their attention and were printed, although the Kings' Sagas were by no means neglected. Verelius' edition of the sagas of Gautrek and Hrolf Gautreksson published in 1664 represents the first saga texts to be printed in the original. It was accompanied by a Swedish translation, as were the other

---

[1] The nationality of this literature has long been a bone of contention between the Icelanders and the Norwegians. Keyser and Munch tried to show that the Kings' Sagas, although perhaps written in Iceland, were virtually composed in Norway. Their theory was never generally accepted and Storm, among others, showed it was untenable. It has, however, been revived in a somewhat different form by Halvdan Koht, but, I believe, without success. I can not help seeing an echo of this theory of his in the title of his otherwise very good book *The Old Norse Sagas* (New York 1931). It is to be remembered that whatever origin the oral saga had, or whatever its subject, the saga as a literary phenomenon is undeniably an Icelandic creation.

editions, like the sagas of Bósi (1666) and of Hervör (1672), and the two editions of Sturlaug's Saga (1697). In 1670 Jón Rugman's translation of the Heimskringla and other Kings' Sagas (*Norlandz Chronika*) appeared, and in 1697 Peringskjöld's edition of the *Heimskringla* with Swedish and Latin versions. Reenhjelm had in 1697 edited in a similar way Odd's Saga of Olaf Tryggvason, and Olaf Rudbeck was also in the field, but the five sagas he edited during the years 1695–97 are now very scarce because almost the whole issue was burned. Several Icelanders were at that time working in Sweden and had a great part in these editions.[1]

During the first decades of the eighteenth century a few other sagas appeared, and in 1737 there finally came from the press E. J. Björner's ponderous tome *Nordiska kämpa dater*, containing sixteen Mythical-heroic Sagas, with Swedish and Latin translations. In 1746 J. Göranson's edition of the *Gylfaginning*, with a long and curious title, made its appearance, and with it came to an end the editorial activity which had lasted for nearly a century.

Interest in this literature, however, continued, and it played a great part in the Romantic movement in Sweden; of this we have an enduring monument in Tegnér's *Frithiof's Saga*, the subject of which he had taken from Björner's work.[2] But only a few texts were printed there during those years. While visiting Stockholm Rask brought out here the two Eddas in 1818, the first complete editions of these famous works. There was an edition of the Saga of the Jomsvikings (1815), and another of the *Heimskringla* (1816–19), a mere reprint of the large Danish edition, as the Swedish edition of 1870–73 was a reprint of Unger's edition. During the last three decades of the eighteenth century Theodor Wisén and Gustaf Cederschiöld were especially active as editors. The former edited the Stockholm *Homilíubók* (1872), one of the oldest of Icelandic texts, a volume of *Riddararímur* (1881), and an anthology of skaldic poetry with a glossary (*Carmina norræna*, 1883–86). Among the works edited by Cederschiöld, the most prominent place must be given to his edition of five Romantic Sagas, under the title *Fornsögur Suðr-*

---

[1] A description of all these editions is to be found in *Islandica* XIV.

[2] Cf. A. B. Benson, *The Old Norse Element in Swedish Romanticism*. New York 1914. 8°.

landa (1877–84) with an excellent introduction. He has, however, several others to his credit, such as those of the sagas of the Jomsvikings (1874), of the Bandamenn (1874), and various others; many of them were published in the year book of Lund University. A few Swedish inaugural dissertations of those years consist of text and translation of Icelandic works, mostly poetry. Editions by Swedish scholars, like Ludvig Larsson, Nataniel Beckman, Emil Olson, and others have generally, however, of late found place in the publications of the *Samfund* (with the long name), or in the *Altnordische Saga-Bibliothek* of which Cederschiöld was one of the founders.

As to translations into Swedish we find that there also the Mythic-heroic Sagas hold a very prominent place. In 1818–19 J. G. Liljegren's *Skandinaviska fornålderns hjeltesagor* appeared, containing three of these sagas. C. G. Kröningswärd's *Nordiskt sago-bibliothek* of 1834 had nine, and V. O. A Bäckman's *Skandinaviska forntids minnen* of 1858, included the sagas of the Volsungs and Gjukungs. Bäckman, however, planned to have this series comprise six volumes, covering many different sagas, but only this volume was published. In 1895 followed A. Ekermann's *Från Nordens forntid*, giving a free translation of nine sagas, including Njal's Saga and that of the Jomsvikings. There have also been juvenile adaptions of these sagas, such as Kata Dalström's book of 1894.

There has not been lacking interest in the family sagas either. C. J. L. Lönberg included the sagas of the Vatnsdælir and the Eyrbyggjar in the first volume of his *Fornnordiska sagor* (1870–73); others were to follow, but the series was discontinued. Most active, however, in this line was A. U. Bååth. Three collections of translations came from his pen. They are: *Fornnordiska sagor* (1886) with three Icelandic sagas, *Från Vikingatiden* (1888, including the sagas of the Jomsvikings and of Hervör),[1] and *Isländska fornsagor i svensk tolkning* (1909–10), which, however, is a second edition of translations, such as that of Njal's Saga (of 1879), and of the collection of 1886. Other translations by Bååth are those of Egil's Saga (1883), of Kormak's Saga (1895), and of the Laxdæla Saga (1900). He has also translated some

---

[1] These two collections have recently been re-edited by Emil Olson under the title *Isländska sagor* (1925), which forms a volume of Bonnier's *Världslitteraturen*.

poetry. Juvenile adaptations have been made of these sagas as well as of the Kings' Sagas in the works of Hedda Anderson (1893–94: *Nordiska fornsagor* and *Nordiska konungasagor*). Worthy of notice are the two anthologies of Old Icelandic literature by R. Steffen (1905) and E. Wessén (1922).

During the last hundred years or so, the *Heimskringla* has been three times translated into Swedish, the most recent being Emil Olson's translation in three volumes (1919–26) with the illustrations of Storm's Norwegian version. Also of this work there are to be found various selections and adaptations.

5. GERMANY. The attention of the German speaking countries which I include under this head, was, as might be expected, first turned to those works of the Old Icelandic literature which deal with the Volsung, or Nibelung, legend and the mythology. In the second decade of the last century Fr. H. von der Hagen and the Grimm Brothers edited and translated separately the heroic lays of the Poetic Edda. The next work of importance to be printed after that was Hermann Lüning's edition of the Poetic Edda (1857). It was, of course, difficult for Germans to edit texts since manuscripts were not easily accessible to them, yet after the middle of the century there appeared quite a few editions. In 1855 came the first edition from the hands of Theodor Möbius (*Elómsirvalla saga*), and there were others to follow, among them one of the Poetic Edda (1860), of Ari's *Íslendingabók* (1869), and of Snorri's *Háttatal* (1879–80). Important also was his anthology, *Analecta norræna* (1855, 2nd ed. 1887) with a glossary (1866), and his two bibliographies of Norse-Icelandic literature (1856 and 1880) were a great help to all workers in this field. With Gudbr. Vigfusson he edited a volume of three Sagas of Icelanders, entitled *Fornsögur* (1860). Konrad Maurer who did so much to further these studies, has only edited the Saga of Gull-Thorir (1858), published on the eve of his visit to Iceland, and the *Skíðaríma* (1869). Fr. W. Bergmann edited and translated many of the Eddic poems, and Eugen Kölbing made a special study of the Romantic Sagas, several of which he edited, beginning with four which were included in a volume styled *Riddarasögur* (1872). Of other collective works especially noteworthy are *Íslenzk ævintýri* (1882–83) edited and translated by Hugo Gering, and *Eddica*

minora (1903) edited by A. Heusler and W. Ranisch. Editions have appeared of various works, especially of the Poetic Edda, which can not all be enumerated here. Most noteworthy are, perhaps, the variorum edition of the Poetic Edda begun by K. Hildebrand and continued by H. Gering, *Zwei Isländerge- schichten*, a model textbook by A. Heusler, and, last but not least, Rudolf Meissner's edition of the *Rómveriasaga* (1910) with an excellent commentary and notes.

In 1886 Max Niemeyer, in Halle, undertook to publish under the editorship of Eugen Mogk a handy series of *Altnordische Texte*, but only two works appeared, viz. Gunnlaug's Saga edited by Mogk, and the Poetic Edda (1888–90) edited by Finnur Jónsson. The series was then discontinued, and another different and more serviceable entered upon by the same firm. This was the *Altnordische Saga-Bibliothek*, under the general editorship of Cederschiöld, Gering, and Mogk. The object of it was to spread the knowledge about the saga literature among German speaking peoples by the publication of annotated editions of the most important sagas of the various groups. The managing editors solicited the collaboration of scholars of other nations, thus making this an international enterprise, although published in German. So far eighteen volumes (1892–1929) have appeared, and it is safe to say that they have been of great value to students of all lands who wished to become acquainted with this literature, whether in the class room or by private study. Of the editors, there were six Germans, three Swedes, one Dane, one Dutchman, one Icelander, and one American. It is to be hoped that the series will be continued.

As translators the Germans have been even more prolific than as editors. The Eddas, especially the Elder, have always been popular with them, and many have tried their hand at rendering them wholly or in part, or even at rewriting them. To mention all such efforts would take too much space, I shall briefly refer to them below. There are, of course, also many other works which have found translators, but I shall here confine myself principally to collective, or serial, publications. Hagen's *Nordische Heldenromane* (1814–15) are the first of this kind. Ludw. Ettmüller gave in his *Altnordische Sagenschatz* (1870) renderings of several of the Mythical-heroic Sagas. In 1875 A. E. Wollheim da Fonseca gave an extensive anthology of all branches of the Icelandic literature in his *Die National-Literatur der Skandinavier*. Karl Küchler gave a translation of three sagas in his *Nordische Heldensagen* (1892). The Kunstwart-Verlag in Munich published in 1907 three volumes by Arthur Bonus entitled *Isländerbuch*, with the subtitle *Sammlung Altgermanischer Bauern- und Königsgeschichten*, the first two of which contain selections from the Sagas of Icelanders, and one of Kings' Sagas, together with a few short tales, while the third volume is filled largely with essays on the saga literature, its significance and value. An one volume selection (*Jugendauswahl*) of this work was later published, and recently portions of this have been issued as separate numbers of the series *Deutsche Jugendbücherei*.

In 1909 appeared in Leipzig the first volume of *Altnordische Erzählungen*, by E. Wilken, containing six of the Eastfjord sagas, but no more was published. In the following year E. Dagobert Schoenfeld's *An nordischen Königshöfen* was published in Strassburg, giving a translation of twenty-eight tales (*þættir*) from the Kings' Sagas, modelled upon the collective edition of these tales of 1904 mentioned above.

The largest undertaking of translations from the Icelandic to be found anywhere is represented by the series *Thule, Altnordische Dichtung und Prosa*, which, under the general editorship of Felix Niedner, began to appear in Jena in 1912, published by Eugen Diederichs of that place. There is an introductory volume by the general editor, dealing with the civilization of Iceland during the Viking Age. The series begins with a new version of the Eddic poems in two volumes by Felix Genzmer, perhaps one of the best in any language, and a few sagas had been printed when the work was interrupted by the war. Soon after peace had been established it was resumed, and in 1930 the twenty-fourth and last volume saw the light. Of this important series vols. III to XIII contain thirty-eight Sagas of Icelanders (including that of the Faroese), vols. XIV–XVI Snorri's *Heimskringla*, vols. XVII–XVIII the other Kings' Sagas together with forty minor tales, vol. XIX the sagas of the Orkneys, the Danish kings, and the Jomsvikings, vol. XX the Prose Edda with the first Grammatical Treatise, vols. XXI–XXII selected heroic sagas, vol. XXIII the sagas of the settlement of Iceland and the early bishop (greatly abridged), and vol. XXIV the Saga of the Sturlungs (also much abridged). Every volume is provided with an introduction, also with maps, where such are required, and many have pictures of places. There are eleven translators, and, as is natural, their work is somewhat uneven, but generally speaking the translating has been well done. There are, of course, exceptions, but corrections will be made in later editions. Some translators have gone so far as to translate all, or most of, the place-names. This has been criticized, and I think justly.[1] By this series there has been placed in the hands of German readers all that is best in Old Icelandic and Old Norse literatures in an intelligible and attractive form. No other country owns a uniform set of the same kind.

Still there is another series of a similar kind, though not so comprehensive. Walter Baetke, one of the translators of the *Thule* series, is the editor of another called *Bauern und Helden, Geschichten aus Alt-Island*, which is published by the Hanseatische Verlagsanstalt in Hamburg. Between 1923 and 1927 eight volumes of this series appeared, containing ten Sagas of Icelanders, each with introduction, maps and pictures of historical sites. The translations are good, made by the general editor and four others, the volumes of a neat appearance and well made up. All this seems to indicate that this literature is popular with the Germans of today.

6. HOLLAND. Several Dutch scholars have made contributions to the study of Old Icelandic literature, but of editions and translations there have not been many. Especially noteworthy, however, is B. Sijmons' edition of the Poetic Edda (1906) with an introduction of permanent value. R. C. Boer also prepared an edition of the Edda (1922) with an historical-critical commentary, and he has besides edited a few sagas, the sagas of Örvar-Odd (1888) and of Björn Hitdælakappi (1893), and two sagas in the *Altnordische Saga-Bibliothek*. Other editions have been prepared at the instance of Boer by his pupils, such as the *Codex Trajectinus* of the Prose Edda by W. van Eden (1913), the Saga of the Kjalnesings by Johanna Posthumus (1911), and the *Hemingsrímur* by Petronella M. den Hoed (1928), all these being published as inaugural dissertations. Of translations there are only two to be noted. E. H. Lasonder

---

[1] In defense of this, see A. Heusler's article in *Mitteilungen der Islandfreunde* VII, 1920, pp. 47–51.

translated the Tale of Thorwald Kodraasson and issued it together with the text (1886), and Jan de Vries translated Gisli's Saga (1925).

7. ENGLAND. It was a mere accident that an Icelandic text was printed in England in the seventeenth century. Christian Worm, while studying at Oxford, had Ari's *Schedæ* printed there in 1696. Although influences from Icelandic literature are manifest in English literary movements,[1] no Icelandic texts were published in England until Dasent's edition of *Theophilus* (1845) which, however, was printed in Sweden nearly thirty years later Eiríkur Magnússon's edition and translation of the *Lilja* (1872) appeared, and others were soon to follow.

The Icelandic dictionary which Richard Cleasby had been working on, was left unfinished at his death. In 1864 his heirs charged Gudbrand Vigfusson with the task of completing it and preparing it for the printer. The Clarendon Press undertook to publish it, and in 1866 Vigfusson moved to Oxford, thus establishing a connection with that institution which has resulted in great service to Icelandic letters. In 1874 the dictionary was published, and I think it is no exaggeration to say that no single book has furthered so much the study of Icelandic language and literature as has this dictionary, not only among the English speaking peoples but elsewhere as well. In 1878 the *Sturlunga saga* was published in two volumes including a brief history of Icelandic literature. In the following year Vigfusson in collaboration with F. York Powell brought out *An Icelandic Prose Reader*, an excellent textbook where some of the selections are derived directly from the manuscripts.[2] And in 1883 their *Corpus Poeticum Boreale* was published covering the Eddic and skaldic poetry with English prose version, and full of all kinds of information. Doubtless it contains many heterodox opinions, also some erroneous and arbitrary conclusions, but the work is conceived on a grand scale, and I know of no other which presents the subject in such an interesting way. so that most people

---

[1] See especially, F. E. Farley, *Scandinavian Influences in the English Romantic Movement*, Boston 1903, viii + 250 pp.; C. E. Herford, *Norse Myth in English Poetry*, Manchester 1919, 31 pp.; and C. H. Nordby, *The Influence of Old Norse Literature upon English Literature*, New York 1901, x + 78 pp.

[2] Modelled upon it is E. V. Gordon's *Introduction to Old Norse*. Oxford 1927.

opening these volumes at random will feel inclined to read on. After the death of both Vigfusson and Powell, their other great work, *Origines Islandicæ*, was published in 1903 in two volumes, a work conceived on similar lines as the *Corpus*, giving the texts, with English translation, relating to the foundation and early history of the Icelandic Commonwealth.   Much harsh criticism has been hurled at this posthumous work, and it is to be regretted that Vigfusson was not alive to answer some of his critics.   Yet in spite of all its shortcomings it is a monumental work, and might well serve as a model for other editors by its presentation of a continuous history and connected literature.   It is un-doubtedly the right way to treat the subject rather than to issue these sagas in isolated editions and at long intervals. Vigfusson was a genius, but frequently an erratic one.   He had a profound knowledge of the subject, and an intellectual grasp of it such as few have shown.   His memory was phenomenal, and relying unduly upon it, he made many mistakes.   His imagination was lively, and he frequently allowed it to carry him beyond proper limits.   He had the power of felicitous expression, and his writings are full of original ideas, and make inspiring reading.

In the Rolls Series are included a few sagas which concern in one way or another the British Isles.   Eiríkur Magnússon edited and translated Thomas' Saga (1875–83), and in 1887 two volumes of *Icelandic Sagas* appeared, edited by Vigfusson, including King Hakon Hakonsson's Saga and the Saga of the Orcadians, a translation of which by Dasent followed in 1894. Elsewhere this phase of Icelandic literature has been treated more recently, viz. in Alan O. Anderson's *Early Sources of Scottish History* (1922) where all passages from Icelandic literature are given in translation, and in Margaret Ashdown's *English and Norse Documents relating to the Reign of Ethelred the Unready* (1930), which gives the original texts with a translation.

In the field of translation the English have been quite active. The poetry seems to have attracted them at first, as evidenced by Thomas Percy's *Five Pieces of Runic Poetry* (1763), Wm. Herbert's renderings in his *Miscellaneous Poetry* (1804–06), and A. S. Cottle's translation of the Edda (1797), but all these probably go back to Latin translations.[1]   The prose literature

---

[1] Some of the risque stanzas of the *Lokasenna* Cottle has left in Latin.

first became known to English readers through Percy's translations of Mallet's *Northern Antiquities* (1779), a work which passed through several, somewhat revised, editions, and through Walter Scott's abstract of the Eyrbyggja Saga (1814). In 1844 appeared Samuel Laing's translation of the *Heimskringla*, which is based on Aall's Norwegian one. George Webbe Dasent came forth at that time, and led the way to the original texts. During his short stay in Sweden in the early forties he brought out a translation of the *Gylfaginning* (1842), and thereupon turned to Njal's Saga, a translation of which he finished nearly twenty years later. His *Story of Burnt Njal* (1861) was well received, and a model translation as it in many ways is, it has become a classic, has passed through many editions and formed a basis for some adaptations. In 1866 Dasent's translation of Gisli's Saga (*The Story of Gisli the Outlaw*) was published, and, as mentioned above, others came later from his pen.

In 1866 Benjamin Thorpe's metrical version of the Elder Edda was published. About that time William Morris became deeply interested in Icelandic literature, visited Iceland twice, and in collaboration with Eiríkur Magnússon produced a number of translations, beginning with the Saga of Grettir (1869), followed by the Story of the Volsungs and the heroic lays of the Edda (1870), *Three Northern Love Stories* (1875), and finally *The Saga Library* in six volumes (London, Quaritch, 1891–1906), the first two containing five Sagas of Icelanders, the rest being devoted to Snorri's *Heimskringla*. Morris' translations are accurate enough, but they are disfigured by archaisms and constructions foreign to the English language. Dasent had tended that way in his first translation, but modified his method later. Vigfusson and Powell unfortunately have also followed this mistaken principle. A readable translation of three Sagas of Icelanders by John Coles, an astronomer, was included in his narrative of a trip to Iceland (1882), and W. C. Green translated Egil's Saga (1893).

In 1892 the Viking Club (afterwards called Society) for Northern Research was founded in London. It has rendered great services to Iceland and its literature, but no text and only a few translations have been published by it. It started a series called *Viking Club Translation Series*, but only two volumes were issued, being translations of Kormak's Saga, with illustrations, by

W. G. Collingwood (1902), and of the mythological poems of the Edda by Olive Bray, also illustrated by Collingwood (1908). No more of this Edda translation was published, because of the death of the translator.

David Nutt, the London publisher, instituted in 1895 a series of translations styled *Northern Library*, and for four years there appeared a volume yearly. This included the sagas of King Olaf Tryggvason and of King Sverrir, both by J. Sephton, the Saga of the Faroese, by F. York Powell, and the late Ambales Saga (*Hamlet in Iceland*), text with translation by Israel Gollancz.

Of other recent translations there may especially be mentioned the two collections by Nora Kershaw (Mrs. Chadwick) entitled *Stories and Ballads of the Past* (1921, including three Mythical-heroic Sagas) and *Anglo-Saxon and Norse Poems* (1922), a prose version with text of the *Hávamál* by Miss Clarke (1923), and translations of the Saga of Grettir by G. Ainslie Hight (1915), and of Egil's Saga by E. R. Eddison (1930), the latter very carefully done but unfortunately marred by too archaic a style in places. The latest addition to English translations is E. Monsen's of the *Heimskringla* (1931), handsomely made up, and apparently based upon Storm's Norwegian version, with the illustrations from it. An attractive little anthology of chapters from the sagas is E. E. Kellett's *The Northern Saga* (1929).

Before leaving the subject of English translations one can not but feel a regret that neither W. P. Ker nor Dame Bertha Phillpotts undertook the translation of any Icelandic work. From translated passages to be found in their writings one gets the impression that they knew the happy medium with regard to style and choice of words, that is neither too modern nor too archaic.

8. AMERICA. Rafn's *Antiquitates Americanæ* aroused much interest in America, and called forth a great number of reviews and articles, but otherwise for a long time little evidence of activity in this field is visible there. Half a century later Rafn's work was, however, supplanted by one of a similar kind, but of a more critical character, edited by an American. Arthur M. Reeves' *The Finding of Wineland the Good* (1890) is from every point of view an excellent work, the Wineland sagas are reproduced in facsimile, with printed text, translation, notes, and an

introduction. Otherwise there are few editions of American origin. A. L. Andrews edited Half's Saga for the *Altnordische Saga-Bibliothek* (1909), Henning Larsen edited an Old Icelandic Medical Miscellany, which is to be found among the publications of the Norwegian Academy of Sciences (1931), and F. S. Cawley prepared a textbook edition of Hrafnkel's Saga (1932). An edition of Ari's *Íslendingabók* was included in the present series. The editions of Old Norwegian texts by G. T. Flom do not fall within the scope of this essay.

Among the earliest American translations are those of two sagas to be found in the *Viking Tales of the North* (1877) and of the Younger Edda (1880), both by R. B. Anderson, the first in collaboration with Jón Bjarnason. The American-Scandinavian Foundation has published very serviceable translations of the two Eddas by A. C. Brodeur (1916) and H. A. Bellows (1923) respectively, and of the Saga of the Volsungs and Ragnar's Saga by Margaret Schlauch (1931). The University of Texas has issued a good translation of the Elder Edda by Lee M. Hollander (1928), Thorstein Veblen translated the Laxdæla Saga (1925), and a translation of two sagas is included in M. Schlauch's *Medieval Narrative* (1928). Fortunately the American translators have kept clear of the affected style of many of the English versions.

Thus there are not many editions and translations to be recorded on this side of the Atlantic, but Icelandic studies are in their initial stage here, and the number of those who take an interest in the subject is on the increase.

9. THE ROMANCE LANGUAGES. In the Romance countries there are no editions to record. The first evidence of interest in Icelandic literature goes back to the seventeenth century when in the days of Cardinal Mazarin there was talk of engaging an Icelander to promote this study in France, negotiations which, however, came to nothing. It was P. H. de Mallet's works, about the middle of the eighteenth century, which introduced the ancient literature to the French. In 1833 Mlle. R. du Puget issued her translation of the Eddas, and about that time Xavier Marmier rendered into French some of the Eddic poems, and through his history of Icelandic literature made the subject better known among his countrymen. As one might

expect it is principally the heroic legends which interested the French, since they are connected with the early history of France. Eugène Beauvois included a rendering of them in his legendary history of the Franks and the Burgundians (1867), and there have been others, the latest being by the Belgian Felix Wagner (1929). Wagner has four other saga translations to his credit, the *Íslendingabók* (1898), Gunnlaug's Saga (1899), Frithjof's Saga (1904), and Egil's Saga (1925). His countryman, Jules Leclercq, published a paraphrase of five Sagas of Icelanders in the *Revue Britannique*. Of Njal's Saga there is a paraphrase by Jules Gourdault (1886), and a translation by Rodolphe Dareste (1896). Fernand Mossé translated the Laxdæla Saga (1914), A. Sauvageot Gunnlaug's Saga (published in the magazine *La vie des peuples*, 1923), and Georges Sautreau the Saga of Saint Olaf by Snorri (1930).

The only translation into Spanish is the rendering by D. A. de los Rios of Puget's French translation of the Eddas (1856).

Italian translations are few and far between. Italo Pizzi included three Eddic poems in his epic anthology of 1877. Tommaso Cannizzaro translated the *Völuspá* (1908), and a few selected verses from the Eddic poems (1893). Giacomo Braun translated the Lay of Thrym (1902). Sigismondo Friedman translated the Saga of the Volsungs (1927), and G. Brunetti six chapters from Njal's Saga (1914).

10. THE SLAVIC LANGUAGES. Although Rafn's *Antiquités Russes* aroused considerable interest among the Russians, and led at least to the publication of an Icelandic grammar in Russian, of texts only the Saga of Hervör has been published in Russia with a long commentary by I. Sharovolski (1906), but of the three volumes planned, the second has not appeared. The Saga of Finnbogi was translated by F. Batiuschkov (1885), and was later included with a translation of three other sagas and four poems in a collection by I. Glazunov (1903). A Russian translation of the Poetic Edda was published in Moscow in 1917, but I have not seen it.

Joachim Lelewel made a translation into Polish of parts of the Eddas. The first edition of this, a slim volume of some seventy pages, was printed in 1807, but as I have never seen it, I do not know exactly what it contains. The second edition of

1828 is much larger, and includes eighteen of the Eddic poems and a version of the Prose Edda visibly based on Resen's edition. A Polish translation of Gisli's Saga by A. Gorski was published in Warsaw in 1931.

Four works have been translated into Czechish, all by Emil Walter, to wit, Gunnlaug's Saga (1919), the Vatnsdæla Saga (1929), the *Gylfaginning* (1929), and Eysteinn Ásgrímsson's *Lilja* (1924).

11. THE FINNO–UGRIC LANGUAGES. To the Hungarians the Old Norse Atli legend would naturally be of interest, and there is also a Hungarian edition by H. Melzl of the *Atlamál* (1882), and a few commentaries on the poem were written. A Hungarian translation of the heroic lays of the Edda, by Gabór Ignácz, has passed through two editions, the second of which (1911) at least is illustrated.

Into Finnish only Gunnlaug's Saga has been translated, said to have been printed about 1927, but I have not seen a copy of it.

II. Individual Works.

It is not without interest to investigate what works of the Old Icelandic literature have been most widely circulated, or in demand, and the only criterion we have with respect to it is the number of editions and translations of each individual work. It is, however, not so easy to give accurate statistics on this point as it looks at first glance, because it is sometimes difficult to determine what should be classed as an edition and translation. There are numerous selections from these works, as well as abstracts and adaptations, to be found in print, and they can hardly be styled editions or translations, yet they must be taken into consideration when we are trying to ascertain the circulation, or popularity, of any of these writings. In the following survey I include only selections, abstracts, or pharaphrases when they are of importance.

And let us begin with the Poetic Edda.[1] Among Nordists it

---

[1] Since I have limited the scope of this essay to Old Icelandic literature, there may be those who will take exception to my including the Eddic poems, on the ground that they are not, or may not be, Icelandic. Whatever the origin of the poems, the collection in the form we have it is Icelandic, and so long as definite proofs are not forthcoming to the contrary, the Edda can properly be styled Icelandic, if not on any other ground than according to

occupies a similar position to that of Hamlet among the theatrical profession. It is said that all actors entertain the ambition some time in their lives to play the part of Hamlet, and so the aspiration of most Nordists and would-be-Nordists seems to be to make an edition of the Edda, or at least, comment in print on some poem, stanza, or line. Needless to say that most of them fail to get beyond the comments. There are some twenty-five complete and eight partial editions of it, all produced in Germanic countries. Of translations there are eight Danish, one Dutch (partial), three complete and four partial English, one French with four others of the heroic lays, nine German [1] and some twelve or more partial ones, one Hungarian (partial), one Italian (partial), one Latin, three Norwegian (two of them partial),[2] one Polish (partial), one Russian (partial, I believe), one Spanish, and six Swedish (and one partial). Of individual poems the most widely published are the *Völuspá*, the *Lay of Thrym*, and the *Song of the Sun* (if this poem is to be counted at all among the Eddic lays).

The Prose Edda has passed through some thirteen editions, but there is only one complete translation of it, namely that into Latin to be found in the Arna-Magnæan edition. All other translations cover merely the *Gylfaginning* and the *Skáldskaparmál*, and generally of the latter only the myths and tales told there. Of such translations there are one Czechish, five Danish, four English, three French, seven German, two Latin, one Polish, one Spanish, and two Swedish. These numbers, however, do not give accurate information about the circulation in print of the myths and tales of Snorri's Edda, because they have been paraphrased and retold over and over again in various languages, and there is a legion of such popular and juvenile books, especially in the Germanic languages.

Turning now to the saga literature, I shall give the figures for some of the Sagas of Icelanders. *Gunnlaug's Saga* leads with

---

the old adage, *Beati possidentes*. I can not see any justification for Finnur Jónsson's talking about "the Norwegian Edda" (see *Greenland*, ed. by M. Vahl, and others, Copenhagen, 1929, II, p. 356), because there is no such work, even though some of the poems may be of Norwegian origin.

[1] Of these, that by Karl Simrock has passed through at least eleven editions, and that by W. Jordan four.

[2] Here and elsewhere I count as Norwegian all translations which have appeared in Norway, irrespective of the idiom they are in.

some twenty-one editions,[1] and of translations there are one Czechish, eight Danish, three English, one Faroese, one Finnish, two French, eight German, five Norwegian, one Latin, and seven Swedish. *Egil Skallagrimsson's Saga* boasts eight editions, four Danish translations, two English, one French, three German, one Latin, two Norwegian, and two Swedish. The *Bandamanna Saga*, eight editions, three Danish translations, three English, one French, three German, and two Norwegian. *Erik the Red's Saga*, nine editions, three Danish translations, five English, one French, three German, one Latin, two Norwegian, and one Russian. The *Eyrbyggja Saga*, six editions, two Danish translations, three English, two German, one Latin, two Norwegian, and one Swedish. *Gisli Sursson's Saga*, eight editions, three Danish translations, one Dutch, one English, four German, three Norwegian, one Polish, and one Swedish. The *Saga of Grettir*, five editions, five Danish translations, five English, two German, one Norwegian, and one Swedish. The *Saga of Hen-Thorir*, eight editions, one Danish translation, two English, three German, and two Norwegian. *Havard's Saga*, seven editions, two Danish translations, two English, three German, and three Norwegian. *Hrafnkel's Saga*, ten editions, five Danish translations, two English, one French, four German, four Norwegian, and two Swedish. The *Laxdœla Saga*, six editions, three Danish translations, three English, one French, five German, one Latin, three Norwegian, and one Swedish. *Njal's Saga*, eight editions, five Danish translations, one English, two French, three German, one Latin, four Norwegian, and two Swedish. Others have fewer, and practically all of them have been translated into one language or another; the only exceptions are the sagas of Gull-Thorir and of the Kjalnesings, which have never been translated. It may be noted that of Ari's *Íslendingabók* there are sixteen editions, one Danish translation, two English, one French, three German, and two Latin. The *Landnámabók* shows thirteen editions (counting the various recensions), two English translations, one Latin, and one greatly abridged German.

Among the Kings' Sagas the *Heimskringla* leads with ten editions, two Danish translations, three English, three German, two Latin, seven Norwegian, and five Swedish. The *Saga of King Sverrir* has five editions, two Danish translations,

---

[1] This number includes the nine editions in Wimmer's *Oldnordisk Læsebog*.

one English, two Latin, five Norwegian, and two Swedish. *Hakon Hakonsson's Saga*, six editions, two Danish translations, one English, five Norwegian, one German, and two Latin. The sagas of the two Olafs have also been often edited and translated, but here we have to distinguish between many different sagas. The *Orkneyinga Saga* has four editions, two English translations, one Latin, and one Norwegian. The *Færeyinga Saga*, six editions, four Danish translations, two English, three Faroese, two German, one Latin, and four Norwegian. The *Saga of the Jomsvikings*, nine editions, four Danish translations, three English, two German, two Latin, one Norwegian, and two Swedish.

Coming now to the Mythical-Heroic Sagas we find that the number of editions and translations decreases. It must, however, be borne in mind that abstracts, or summaries, of several of these sagas are quite numerous, and they are not included as a rule in the figures given here. *Frithjof's Saga* owes its popularity principally to Tegnér's famous poem which is based upon it; it boasts eleven editions, one Danish translation, five English, one French, eight German, one Latin, two Norwegian, and eight Swedish. *Hervarar Saga* has ten editions, four Danish translations, one French, one English, four German, one Latin, and three Swedish. *Ragnar's Saga*, five editions, two Danish translations, three German, one English, one Latin, one Norwegian, and three Swedish. The *Saga of the Volsungs* shows ten editions, two Danish translations, three English, two French, six German, one Italian, two Norwegian, and one Swedish.

The Skaldic poems with their rigid and intricate metrical rules and wealth of circumlocutions present no easy subject for the translator to attack. It is virtually impossible to represent their peculiar art in a translation, although their meaning can be conveyed easily enough. So artificial a poetry becomes generally insipid in any other language than the original one. We have two collected editions of these poems, by Vigfusson and Powell, and by Finnur Jónsson, with prose versions in English and Danish respectively. For a long time it was a favored occupation of philologists to compile lengthy commentaries on these poems and the Icelanders took there the leading part; this went so far at last, as almost to obscure the more attractive and important qualities of this literature. Of late these studies have been revived on a broader linguistic and literary basis, and seemingly with promise of better results, as shown by the works of E. A. Kock in Sweden, and Felix Genzmer and Konstantin Reichardt in Germany, and furthermore by the publication of a special textbook with glossary (*Skaldisches Lesebuch*, 1931) by Kock and Rudolf Meissner.

In spite of all the difficulties with which translators have to contend, attempts have not been lacking to make metrical versions of these poems. I might especially mention here two small volumes of translations into Swedish by Aksel Åkerblom (*Nordiska fornkväden*, 1899, and *Norræna dikter*, 1916), and one by E. Hellquist (*Dikter av äldre och nyare germanska skalder*, 1924), and translators of the sagas have usually had to try their hand at rendering the stanzas found there, naturally with varying success. The poems of Egil Skallagrimsson and Sighvat Thordsson are seemingly those which have found most translators.

One of the most widely read and translated poems is the *Krákumál*, or the *Death Song of Ragnar Lodbrok*. This poem which probably was written in Iceland in the twelfth century became known early through Latin translations, and was especially admired in the days of Romanticism. There are, at least, a dozen editions of it, five Danish translations, one Dutch, six English, one French, five German, one Italian, four Latin, one Norwegian, one Russian, and three Swedish.[1] Of the early Christian poetry Eystein Ásgrimsson's *Lilja* occupies the foremost place; it has been printed many times, and boasts one Czechish translation, one Danish, one Flemish, one French, two German, two Latin, one Norwegian, and one Swedish.

The *Darrad Lay* of Njal's Saga, and the *Hervör Lay*, or the *Awakening of Angantyr*, as it is often called, of Hervarar Saga, have tempted many translators, but they are of the Eddic type.[2]

III. Printing. Illustrations.

With regard to the printing and make-up of editions there are few things of particular interest to be recorded. It has not been customary to issue any *editions de luxe*—the expense of issuing an ordinary edition has generally been found burdensome

[1] Cf. *Islandica* V, pp. 36–39.

[2] Cf. *Islandica* I, pp. 84–85; V, pp. 24–25.

enough, so extra cost was seldom incurred for the sake of beauty. What strikes us in the case of many of the early editions is their size. They are frequently in quarto and sometimes in folio. This was probably partly done to impress people, partly directed by necessity, because usually a large type was used, and a translation and glossary were often included; sometimes there was padding of various kinds in the way of notes and explanatory treatises, and thus a short saga like that of Gunnlaug could swell up to a quarto volume of nearly five hundred pages. It was Rafn who introduced the octavo as the usual size of editions, and showed there as elsewhere his practical sense. Big volumes are not easily read and handled, and Rafn intended his publications for readers, although occasionally he thought it advisable to impress people by large, heavy tomes. Probably the handsomest among editions is that by Reeves of the Wineland Sagas. Especially noteworthy are the Munksgaard facsimile editions and their very attractive make-up.

It is among the translations that we often find well printed volumes. The original edition of Dasent's translation of the *Story of Burnt Njal* (1861) is very pleasing with regard to printing, paper, and binding. Morris and Magnússon's version of the *Saga of the Volsungs*, and their *Three Northern Love-Stories* printed in 1901 at the Chiswick Press, are a delight to the eye. Of other English translations, that of the Edda by Bray, that of Kormak's Saga, by Collingwood, and the recent one of the *Heimskringla* by Monsen, are all attractive. As to typography the little volume containing the *Saga of Hen-Thorir*, printed at the Byway Press in Cincinnati (1903), is interesting. Of Danish translations that by Gjellerup of the Edda takes the first place, and the new three-volume one of the Sagas of Icelanders makes a very good impression. The Swedish and Danish editions of Gödecke's rendering of *Ragnar's Saga* impresses by its large size, clear type and good illustrations. The large edition of Storm's translation of the *Heimskringla* is exceedingly well done from every point of view, and even the octavo editions of it are in very good taste. The quarto edition of Mortensen's *Edda-kvæde* is likewise very attractive. Olson's Swedish translation of the *Heimskringla* is a fine example of typography and make-up. And from all these rather large volumes we finally come to dainty little ones like Ritter's French adaptation of the Volsung lays (*Sigurd*, 1897) and the recent edition of Wagner's translation of *Gunnlaug's Saga* (1925).[1]

As the medieval scribe found it desirable to have his manuscript illuminated, so the modern publisher, editor, or translator, often wants the printed book provided with illustrations of one kind or another. We can find indications of this even in the earliest printed texts. Verelius had a portrait of the great king placed on the back of the title-page of the fragmentary Olaf's Saga which he edited (1665), and in the Skalholt edition of sagas we find anonymous woodcuts representing King Olaf Tryggvason and Erik the Red which we sincerely hope do not show the true likenesses of these doughty heroes. Gunnlaug's Saga of 1775 includes, besides two plates showing the interior of old Icelandic houses, three small copper engravings depicting incidents in the saga.

The artistic representations of Old Northern and Old Icelandic subjects were slow in developing and beset with many pitfalls. We are concerned here only with those which appeared in printed editions and translations of Icelandic works. The subjects which the artists first tried their hand at were those of mythology and heroic legends, and there it proved difficult for them to establish a style and form independent of classical art. Early in the nineteenth century there occurred a somewhat acrimonious controversy about the suitability of subjects from Norse mythology for artistic representation. It was not of much importance, though those who took the positive side in the discussion got rather the better of it. It is not, however, until after the middle of that century that pictures of this kind commence to show signs of independent treatment, Northern atmosphere and characteristics. Among the most successful artists was Lorenz Frølich, whose exquisite pen drawings adorn the pages of Gjellerup's translation of the Edda. There is life and character in these pictures, although objections have been raised to their nudity, not on moral, but on traditional grounds. A different type is represented by Louis Moe's illustrations in the Danish rendering of some Edda tales by S. T. Thyregod (1890); they represent many attractive features

---

[1] I have not seen an expensive, and apparently very pretentious, edition of a German translation of the *Lay of Völund*, with woodcuts by Joseph Weiss, recently published in Offenbach a. M.

and fertile imagination.   Less successful seem to me the illustrations by twenty Swedish artists in Sander's Edda translation
(1893). Of illustrations in popular adaptations of mythical and
heroic tales, there is no end in Scandinavia, as well as in other
countries, especially Germany and England, but very few of
these are of particularly noteworthy character, although not infrequently they are fairly well done.[1] No one will, however,
longer doubt that these subjects are not only suitable for, but
very tempting, to artists and illustrators.

In mythological pictures artists can give their imagination
freer play, provided the right atmosphere is observed. They
are more restricted in their representations of subjects from the
historical sagas, and even of those in certain heroic sagas. There
historical accuracy is expected with respect to dress and other
items. So long as there was not sufficient archæological material
to build upon, illustrations in this kind of writings were very
indifferent, as those in Gunnlaug's Saga mentioned above show.
Probably the earliest satisfactory illustrations of this character
are those by Otto Bache, the Danish painter, which he made for
his brother's history of the North (1867–76). It is, however,
especially Norwegian artists who have excelled here. The
illustrations by A. Bloch in Rolfsen's *Vore Fædres Liv* (1898)
are well drawn and convey the impression of reality. Unsur-
passed are the contributions of six Norwegian artists to Storm's
translation of the *Heimskringla* (1899), drawings full of life and
movement. They have now been given a wider circulation by
being included in Olson's Swedish version and Monsen's English.
In various Swedish translations have appeared illustrations by
Jenny Nyström-Stoopendaal; they are generally pleasing, but
have a tendency to smoothness and idealization, often not quite
in conformity with the subject. Very interesting are A.
Malmström's illustrations in Gödecke's rendering of Ragnar's
Saga (1880).

Artists of other lands, illustrating works dealing with this
period, often hark back to the times when the Vikings were
pictured as villainous looking brutes with hanging moustache or
flowing beard, crowned by horned or winged helmet. At other

[1] Cf. P. Johansen, *Nordisk Oldtid og dansk Kunst*, København 1907; A.
Sterner, *Om den nordiska mytens använding i bildande konst*, Stockholm 1881;
Paul Herrmanowski, *Die deutsche Götterlehre und ihre Verwertung in Kunst und
Dichtung*, II. Bd., Berlin 1891.

times the reverse is observed. Thus C. E. St. John Mildmay's illustrations in Dasent's translation of Gisli's Saga lack altogether the Northern vigor and severity. V. Stuyvaert's woodcuts in the last edition of Wagner's translation of Gunnlaug's Saga also have an exotic atmosphere.

No Icelanders have as yet attempted illustrating the histories and lives of their ancestors. It is to be hoped that when they learn the art of illustration, they may represent historical characters and scenes from the native sagas in proper settings and in full harmony with the surroundings.

And this brings us to another kind of illustrations, the strictly historical ones, that is, pictures of historical places and scenery, as well as of archæological remains and the like. They are of great value and necessary aids for the proper understanding of this literature. The first work to be illustrated in this way is Aall's translation of the *Heimskringla* (1838–39) which has beautiful steel engravings from Flintoe's pictures of various historical places. Many recent works now show such things in reproductions from photographs, as some of the volumes in the *Thule* collection and in *Bauern und Helden,* and they often give satisfaction.

In this kind of illustrations two artists are especially prominent. In the summer of 1897 W. G. Collingwood, the English artist and archæologist, made a trip to Iceland for the purpose of making sketches and aquarelles of historical places there. Many of these were published in his and Jón Stefánsson's *A Pilgrimage to the Saga-Steads of Iceland* (1899) and in their translation of Kormak's Saga (1902). I know of no pictures which give a better idea of the Icelandic landscape than these. They show it under various aspects, and the aquarelles display the great variety of colors which one often observes there. Of course, we get only the summer atmosphere, not that of winter, which is of equal interest. In 1927, Johannes Larsen, the Danish artist, spent the summer in Iceland, in order to make the illustrations for the Danish translation of sagas which was then in preparation. These pen and ink drawings have now appeared, and in spite of the great technical skill they indicate, I must confess that to me most of them are disappointing. They do not really convey the atmosphere of the Icelandic landscape. They frequently show a vagueness of outline, although sometimes the contours may be somewhat exaggerated. And the general impression is apt to be that of monotony. The difference between Larsen and Collingwood is marked, and probably largely due to their previous experience. Larsen, a native of Denmark, where forests and soft contours predominate, and which he is used to sketching, found a totally different environment in Iceland from that with which he was familiar. On the other hand, Collingwood, a devotee of mountains and long resident of the Lake District, found in Iceland similar conditions to those his eye was accustomed to, mountains and crags, rivers and lakes, and he was in a position to reproduce these feelingly and faithfully. In this lies largely, I believe, the superiority of his illustrations to those of Larsen.

IV. Epilogue.

The foregoing survey shows sufficiently, I believe, that the Old Icelandic literature finds favor with various groups of modern readers of many lands. The number of editions and translations bears out this view. The publication of such books, however, has been by fits and starts. There is no organization which for any great length of time has undertaken to supply them to the public in a systematic and attractive way. Societies have been formed, have displayed considerable activity for a while, and then have relinquished their efforts, been dissolved, or switched into some other field. A few publishing-houses have been more consistent and methodical in their efforts, and thus rendered very valuable service to this literature. Among publishers may be mentioned especially Sigurdur Kristjánsson, in Iceland, Max Niemeyer and Eugen Diederichs in Germany, the Clarendon Press in England, and, last but not least, Levin & Munksgaard in Denmark, whose publications, only recently started, promise to be of fundamental importance.

It has been the misfortune of the Icelanders that they have had neither the means nor the facilities themselves to publish all these writings of their ancestors so that function has been performed principally by the sister nations in the North. Unfortunately, however, the latter nations have been far too eager in their efforts to prove that the Icelandic literature really was more or less their own. The Swedes at the beginning called it

Old Swedish, the Danes called it Old Northern ('Old Danish' at the time was out of the question), and the Norwegians style it Old Norwegian, or Old Norse. Old Icelandic was a term seldom heard, and then generally *sotto voce*. The societies engaged in publishing these writings generally bore the epithet of Old Northern, and to justify this title they published from time to time some texts of the other countries which were of interest only to a few scholars, while the writings by which the societies virtually existed were all of Icelandic origin, the others being drugs on the market. And this association of the Icelandic literature with the medieval literatures of the other Northern countries, caused the Icelandic to be treated in exactly the same way as they were, the principal stress being laid upon the philological side of it, and thus the recognition of its literary value was delayed.

Another cause for the delay in a proper recognition of this literature is to be sought in the manner in which the works were published. They were generally not grouped together, or published in a sequence, so as to show their relationship. Rafn saw the value of such a grouping and initiated three series of sagas, but this grouping has been later abandoned by the societies, although adopted by some of the publishing firms mentioned above. The trouble with the societies which have devoted themselves to the publication of these texts is that they seldom gave any thought to the public, they were usually thinking of the mere linguistic students, and the chaotic methods which at the present day still exist in the *Samfund* (of the long name) are a good illustration of this neglect. The directors of these societies seldom seem to have given it a thought that what they were publishing might get a much wider circulation, if properly handled, and thus advance the very cause for which the societies themselves had been formed and were maintained.

The editing of the texts has naturally varied. The earliest editions frequently were uncritical, but the method adopted by the Society of Northern Antiquaries was adequate for most purposes. Other societies and editors have followed similar methods. Then the diplomatic editions came into vogue, and philologists eagerly welcomed them. All texts were to be published, if possible, in that way. Doubtless various things can be brought forward in favor of such reproductions, but they have one very serious drawback: most of them are absolutely unreadable, and that can hardly be called a recommendation for any book, because most books are printed to be read. Philologists, however, were supposed to read them, but now we hear testimonies to the contrary and the effort required is said to be too great even for them.[1] In other words, there is no longer much excuse for them. Wherever it is desirable, or necessary, to reproduce old texts accurately there is only one way to do it—by the photographic method, and Mr. Munksgaard has shown the way by his excellent reproductions of manuscripts. Such reproductions are the only absolutely reliable ones from every point of view. But they are for libraries, museums, the scholar and the bibliophile. When the works are of general interest, as are most of the sagas, readable editions are required (with or without variant readings as the case may be), and stress should be laid upon supplying them. Strange as it may seem, for some of the sagas there are no readable editions in existence, not even of those which would be widely read. As an example I might mention the *Morkinskinna*, a collection of kings' sagas full of interesting and well-told tales. Of this there are two editions of the diplomatic type, both virtually unreadable by most mortals, especially the second; but a readable one does not as yet exist.

Still, as a rule, there is no lack of editions, they sometimes multiply unnecessarily, occasionally, as it seems, quite contrary to good reason. There are many examples of uncalled-for editing and re-editing, and many of the books are pleasing neither to eye nor mind, while frequently editions of the proper kind are lacking. There are at present in Copenhagen three organizations which devote more or less of their activities to the publication of Icelandic texts. We should expect that they would divide the field between them and follow one or another principle in selecting works for publication. If they do, it can not be detected. Their publications seem to come out in a haphazard way, according to some inscrutable choice. Most of them fall

---

[1] Finnur Jónsson, the most prolific producer of diplomatic editions, recently confessed that he has come to the conclusion that these editions are not worth while because even the philologists do not read them, but rely for the most part upon the analysis of the orthography generally found as an introduction to the editions (see *Skírnir*, vol. CV, 1931, pp. 14–15).

on deaf ears, partly because they are nowhere advertised. I once asked a prominent member of these organizations why their publications were never advertised. He replied, that as publishers they relied upon reviews in learned periodicals in order to secure circulation for their books. That method may do very well with widely reviewed books, but for the moment I do not recall having seen a review of any of the publications of these three organizations in a learned periodical, or elsewhere, for the last decade, or so, a fact which seems to indicate that they have at least created no sensation.

And this instance is typical of the conditions that exist at present within this field, that is, an absolute lack of a general organization, and of coordination of any kind. Many men in various countries are deeply interested in this subject, but no efforts are made to bring them together, and thus to advance Icelandic studies, as is done nowadays in all other branches of science and learning. The Society of Northern Antiquaries aimed at such an organization, and accomplished much, but unfortunately changed over to another field. To all who have these studies at heart, it must be evident that some kind of central organization is needed as a bond of union between scholars and readers of all lands who are interested in the subject. It would seem most natural that such organization should have its headquarters in Iceland, and for many reasons that would be desirable. But Iceland is somewhat out of the way, also lacks various facilities which are necessary for a centre of publishing activities, such as good libraries; and, I regret to say, frequently the Icelanders, unless spurred on by urgings from without, are rather slow and dilatory, the reasons lying in the fact that they are so far away, and out of touch with other people. Accordingly, I think that some other place would be preferable as the seat of the organization. All in all, Copenhagen probably possesses the best qualifications for it; it lies centrally, has the best collections of Icelandic manuscripts, has good libraries, has academic, commercial, and political connections with Iceland, and, last but not least, possesses a foundation, now about two centuries old, which from the beginning seemed destined to become a centre for these studies and to act as a bond of union between students of all lands. I refer, of course, to the Arna-Magnæan Foundation.

It was founded in 1730 by Árni Magnússon,[1] but did not receive its charter until 1760, as the Danes were slow in recognizing its importance, and probably never have realized its potentialities as a centre for Icelandic studies. About the time it was chartered it had a fund of some 34,000 Danish Kroner, which now has increased to some 65,000 Kroner; from another source the Foundation has received a legacy which makes the whole fund owned by it about 85,000 Kroner. From these figures it is evident that the fund has not grown fast, although yearly a certain amount of the annual income is to be added to the principal. It has been in the hands of a Commission, generally of five members, elected for life. It was, at first, stipulated that two of them should be professors in the University of Copenhagen; the others need not be connected with that institution. Of late, however, it has been customary to choose all from among the professors there. The charter, framed by men who had little knowledge of the subject, is a rather clumsy document; it is easy to understand that most of its provisions are now a dead letter, as indeed they long have been. Yet its original spirit has been preserved; it is one of aloofness and exclusiveness. The corporation was to be a closed one, the publications were to be prepared by the stipendiaries and secretaries, or by the members of the Commission; no other persons were desired. The Commission meets usually once a year to decide about the next year's publication, but not infrequently the annual meeting has been dispensed with and sometimes no minutes have been taken of the other meetings.[2] Not infrequently among the members of the Commission there have been men not only without any particular knowledge of the subject concerned, but even, as it seems, without interest in it.[3] The work has mostly been done by the secretaries, who were not members of the Commission. Most of them have been Icelanders. Although during its existence of two hundred years, the Commission has published between thirty and forty works, one fails to discover any really definite principle in its publishing.

---

[1] See *Islandica* XIX, pp. 58–71.—For the history of the Foundation, see Finnur Jónsson, *Árni Magnússon, Levned og Skrifter*, 1930, I, pp. 199–229, 115–153.

[2] Finnur Jónsson, *op. cit.*, p. 201.

[3] Finnur Jónsson, *op. cit.*, p. 199.

Certainly the provisions of the charter have not been closely observed. Some of the publications are important, although many are now antiquated. Almost from the beginning it has been felt that the Commission was not doing what was expected of it, and for that reason other societies were formed to do the publishing which it failed to do. This rivalry never spurred the Commission to a greater activity. It continued in its desultory way, seemingly oblivious of the changes which were taking place in the world. It published books from time to time, but was apparently indifferent as to the sale, or circulation, of them. The same indifference has shown itself in the supervision of the manuscript collection and the library in the charge of the Commission. The manuscripts have not received proper care, and the founder's library has totally disappeared, some of the books being now in other public libraries. Aloofness, which often is but another name for indifference, and lack of progressive spirit, or of any desire to keep abreast with the time, have been traits characteristic of the Commission throughout these many years. These are, however, faults more or less inherent in most commissions with lifelong memberships. Such commissions usually become impervious to change, or reform, and so stagnate.

Yet, this rather inactive body might be altered into an efficient institution of the kind I mentioned above, and at a comparatively small expense. A new charter would have to be made, and, of course, the lifelong memberships must be abolished; they are inimical to any progressive, prolonged activity. I have elsewhere discussed the question of reorganization.[1] The Foundation is in fact Icelandic, established by an Icelander with his means, and the material was collected by him, mostly in Iceland; but it is in Denmark as a part of the University. Thus nothing could be more becoming than that the Foundation should be governed by a commission composed of Danes and Icelanders in equal numbers, and elected for a certain number of years. In former times it presented difficulties if members lived far apart, but with our means of communication, it is no longer impossible to have members of the same commission, which need not meet often, residing in distant places such as Denmark and Iceland. That is a common practice here in America, where members of the same commission reside anywhere between the Atlantic and

---

[1] See my article in *Skírnir* (vol. II, 1929, pp. 1–35).

the Pacific. The presiding officer should be a Dane, but the secretary, who would also be the director of publications, could be either Icelandic or Danish. And the principal changes to take place would be as follows:[1] Firstly, the former aloofness and exclusiveness should be abandoned and works of merit published within the subjects covered by the Foundation, editions, translations, or other writings, by whomsoever written, preferably in one of the great languages, and provisions made so that these publications became known to those who are interested wherever situated, and this can generally be done by judicious advertising. The editing and re-editing of texts cannot go on forever, it is often merely diverting the money from other urgent uses. Secondly, a periodical publication should be issued, probably a small annual, giving a report of the Foundation's activities and including besides short reviews, essays, or studies dealing with topics of particular interest. Such a periodical is very valuable in order to keep constantly in touch with the public.[2] Thirdly, a library should be formed which included so far as possible the Old Icelandic literature and what has been written about it. It may seem late in the day to begin this, but probably duplicates might be obtained from various public libraries, or from private persons, and books obtained through exchange of publications. Apparently the authors of the charter had something similar in mind, because it provides for an exchange of publications, but this the Commission has disregarded. When such a library has once been established, authors would soon begin to send presentation copies. It may require some time before a library of considerable size can be brought together, but in the meantime a reference catalogue should be compiled on cards of the whole subject in question, so that any one wishing

---

[1] I consider one thing, perhaps, most imperative for the Commission to do, although it does not directly concern the plan I have here in mind, and therefore I consign it to a footnote. It is to restore as far as possible the library left by Árni Magnússon. In the charter it is enumerated among the duties of the Commission to visit this library every third year and to see to it that it is kept in proper condition. It was, however, dispersed long ago, and probably quite a few of its books may still be traced and recovered. No more unpardonable sin can be committed against the shades of a great bibliophile and book collector than to let his collections, which he bequeathed to the public, be dispersed. And Árni was one of the greatest collectors the North has seen.

[2] A very appropriate title of such an annual would be *Arna-Magnæana*.

information might find it there. Besides it might be of aid and guidance for the Commission itself in its deliberations and actions. Such a record is of great and varied importance in many respects, and nothing would be more in the spirit of Árni Magnússon. He himself during his lifetime was eager to collect such things. And after all it would be comparatively easy to make with the aid of various bibliographies. In this way the Arna-Magnæan Foundation would become a centre for these studies, and a worthy monument to the great scholar and collector. To keep it stationary as has been done hitherto, is to act contrary to the founder's spirit. He laid a great foundation upon which he must have expected a structure would be erected which served those interests he had at heart and furthered them.

I do not mean to say that editing of old texts should be abandoned, or neglected, but only that it should be done after some plan, not in a haphazard way. There are many writings which have not yet been edited, and which it would be desirable to have in print. Others may well remain in manuscript. Many other works and studies, however, await publication, and some of these can hardly be made without collaboration or concerted efforts of some kind. Funds for publication may not be so easily obtained in the future as in the past. All nations are going through a financial crisis the end and consequences of which can not as yet be seen. Pecuniary difficulties are affecting our work as they do everything else. And there are other crises and problems to be faced, especially by the small nations.

Among these small nations are the Icelanders. They have preserved perhaps better than any other nation of their size the records of the past, and not only of their own people but also of the other nations in the North. Their land, literature, language, customs, and folklore are rich sources of information about the past, by no means fully explored. As yet the Icelanders have no adequate written history of their land, and in this point lag behind their sister nations in the North, which have many histories. But their own inability to collaborate is to blame for that. The language they have preserved through a thousand years, and as yet it has not been adequately studied and recorded. It is here probably that there is most urgent need for action. The remoteness from other countries and the people's devotion to their own early literature have been the most important factors in preserving the mother tongue. The situation is now changing. We live in the age of aviation, the radio, the talking films, and other inventions which shorten distances and carry words through the air. Listening to speeches and music from foreign lands is now of daily occurrence in thousands of homes in Iceland, and every day thousands of people listen to foreign sound films. All this is bound to affect in a short time their language, thoughts, and habits. And it is therefore necessary to study these before any radical changes have taken place. A historical dictionary of the Icelandic language, and study of the popular idioms, are things which are greatly needed, and can only be done through collaboration and organized effort. This is a task which lies nearest to the Icelanders themselves to undertake. In all other fields of their national culture and literature cooperation with interested foreigners is not only desirable but necessary. I believe that an organization of the kind I have suggested would be of the utmost importance both for furthering the study of these matters and for awakening a more widespread interest in them.